LIFE IN
A MEDIEVAL
CASTLE

FROM 1066 TO THE 1500s

BRIAN WILLIAMS

Manorbier Castle in
Pembrokeshire; the ideal
home according to the
medieval historian Gerald of
Wales, and one of the most
attractively sited castles in
the British Isles.

IMPORTANT DATES

1066   The Normans invade Anglo-Saxon England; William the Conqueror begins building stone castles to guard the conquered kingdom.

1075   The first tower of Windsor Castle is built.

1078   Foundations of the Tower of London are laid.

1086   Domesday Book, Williams the Conqueror's survey of his new realm.

1093   Queen Margaret of Scotland dies in Edinburgh Castle, built by her husband Malcolm Canmore.

1100   Ranulf Flambard, Bishop of Durham, is the first state prisoner held in the Tower of London, on the orders of Henry I – but escapes.

1110   Windsor Castle is first used as a royal residence, by Henry II.

1189   Dover Castle is completed, the last of the great square Norman keeps.

1215   King John is forced to grant Magna Carta to the barons.

1266   The siege of Kenilworth Castle, during Simon de Montfort's revolt against Henry III.

1277   Edward I of England invades Wales; castles such as Caernarfon and Conwy are built to command the coast and river valleys.

1295   At Beaumaris Castle work starts on a dock for seagoing ships. Several Welsh castles had such quays.

1314   Battle of Bannockburn; the Scots under Robert the Bruce defeat the English.

1337–1453   The Hundred Years' War between England and France.

1348   The Black Death strikes Britain.

1381   The Peasants' Revolt, led by Wat Tyler.

1386   Bodiam Castle, one of few English castles erected quickly in a single style.

1390s   Geoffrey Chaucer writes his *Canterbury Tales*. His son Thomas is rich enough to acquire Donnington Castle in Berkshire.

1415   Henry V wins the Battle of Agincourt in France.

1455–85   The Wars of the Roses between York and Lancaster factions in England.

1464   Bamburgh Castle falls after an assault by cannon, the first English castle to be breached by gunfire.

1476   William Caxton sets up the first printing press in London.

1485   Battle of Bosworth Field; the death of Richard III and the crowning of the first Tudor king of England, Henry VII.

1500s   Henry VIII of England builds coastal forts against invasion.

THE MEDIEVAL CASTLE

The medieval castle was fortress and lordly residence, the epitome of secular power. Its stone walls and towers dominated the locality – as was their builders' intention. From the Norman Conquest of 1066 through to the reigns of Tudors in England and Stuarts in Scotland in the 16th century, castles were essential cogs in the slow-grinding wheels of the medieval state, and the focus for a community that maintained the castle and was supported – and at times protected – by it.

Though many castles are now ruins, stranded by the flowing tides of history, others still stand proud as residences, leisure and conference centres, and museums, reminding us that for 500 years the castle was part of the fabric of society, its importance extending beyond the military to the economy, law and social life. England, Scotland, Ireland and Wales have a rich medieval heritage, with castles, large and small, surviving often in unexpected places. Each has a distinct appeal to the visitor. As we climb steps worn smooth by generations of feet, or stand on wind-scoured battlements to peer down into grassed-over moats or mysterious fern-shrouded recesses, it is not easy to picture the castle as a home and place of work, full of bustle and life. Archaeology and scholarship enable us to recapture the essence of the lives spent within such walls, and explore a world more vibrant than the silent, mossy stones of those castles now in ruins might suggest.

A fine example of a medieval castle: Dover Castle in Kent, for centuries the guardian of perhaps the key route for any potential invader.

THE AGE OF CASTLES

The Norman invaders brought stone castles to Britain, after 1066. There had been fortified settlements long before: Celtic Iron Age hillforts, Roman army fortresses, and Anglo-Saxon walled towns or burhs. But the medieval castle played a unique role in the life of local communities for some 500 years.

The Normans in England rapidly secured their conquest with wooden stockades enclosed by banks and ditches, and with timber-built halls, watch-towers and soldiers' quarters inside. From these evolved a chain of castle strongholds – the Round Tower at Windsor dates from about 1175, the shell keep at Launceston Castle in Cornwall from about 1080.

In the 35 years following their victory over the English at Hastings, the Normans built around 200 castles. In theory at least, the king owned them all, for everyone in the realm – from noble to peasant – owed their lands and loyalty to him, but each castle became a personal and family stronghold. Its owner, a nobleman or lord (also known as a baron), managed his lands in the name of the king, raised soldiers in time of war, imposed law and order, and collected taxes from the people under his sway.

Such 'private' castles were costly to maintain, but protected, and were supported by, their local communities – people working inside the castle walls and in farming villages around it. Even a small castle involved a lot of work and expense for its upkeep and defences. Wooden castles did not last; they were liable to rot or catch fire, and so it was worth the effort and expense of reconstruction – to quarry, cart and raise stones, and build permanent fortress-homes. The Normans did this with gusto, and the stone castle became a symbol of their power and the subjugation of those they had overcome. Between 1100 and the early 1500s, castle-architects devised ever-more complex and costly ways to make castles increasingly difficult for an enemy army to capture, borrowing the best ideas in fortification design from across Europe, North Africa and the Near East. The apogee of British fortress design was the concentric castle of the 1300s, with two or more ring-walls encircling the central stronghold, epitomized by the mighty Welsh castles built by Edward I, king of England from 1272 to 1307. In the Wars of the Roses (1455–85) in England, most battles were fought in the open, not in castles, and by this time cannon offered a serious new threat to stone walls; as a result the castle began to look less useful as a fortress. Some castles were turned into more comfortable residences, with a continuing nod towards defensive capability; redundant castles were allowed to crumble and decay.

In its heyday, the castle was one of the most enduring symbols of medieval life, along with the Church – for in the Middle Ages everyone in Britain was at least in name Christian, and there was but one Church, governed from Rome. For most poor people daily life meant hard toil from dawn until dusk, and the towering castle walls were a constant reminder of their lowly place in the social hierarchy. Yet there was colour and chivalry too, as knights rode out in splendid panoply and banners fluttered over high towers. In times of peace and plenty, when cattle were fat and fields were fruitful, there was feasting and fun. Castles stood for temporal power, the enduring hold of king and nobleman over their people. Their stone walls stood for stability in a world of work, war and pestilence, from which Heaven alone promised ease.

▲ The Round Tower at Windsor Castle. It was the first part of the stone fortress erected during the reign of Henry II on the site of William the Conqueror's timber structure.

THE GOOD LIFE

The well-ordered castle fulfilled medieval ideas of the good life and the chivalric ideal, protecting the blessings of peace and prosperity. The chronicler Gerald of Wales (c.1146–1223) extolled the merits of his birthplace, Manorbier Castle in South Wales, which he wrote was 'excellently well defended by turrets and bulwarks', but also had a fine fish pond, orchard and vineyard. The green Pembrokeshire countryside it guarded was 'well supplied with corn, sea-fish and imported wines'.

CASTLE RESIDENTS

After the Norman Conquest of 1066 some English writers lamented freedom lost, manacled by the invaders' castle walls. William I built rapidly in the years after his victory over Harold, raising castles as far north as Newcastle upon Tyne (1080), castles imposed to subdue and awe. The castle owners at first showed the iron fist more often than the velvet glove, but as time passed an Anglo-Norman compromise emerged, and castle residents in England and Scotland settled down and were assimilated into local ways. In Wales and Ireland the castle owner continued to symbolize foreign domination for some time to come.

◀ Harold I slain at Hastings in 1066, as depicted in the Bayeux Tapestry. The king was the heart of medieval power: whoever killed the king would usually win the battle – and the realm.

▲ Dunvegan Castle, ancestral home of the clan MacLeod, is said to be the oldest continuously inhabited castle in Scotland.

Some castles have long housed generations of the same family. Dunvegan Castle on the Isle of Skye has been home to the MacLeods of MacLeod for eight centuries, while Berkeley Castle in Gloucestershire has been in the same family's care since Robert Fitzharding built the first keep in the 12th century. Medieval kings used castles as bases for dynastic manoeuvres, as well as imposing residences: Henry I prudently moved into Windsor Castle to safeguard his shaky hold on the Crown following the mysterious death in 1100 of his brother William II (Rufus). Just as shrewdly, Henry locked up his brother Robert, a potential rival.

Windsor Castle's oldest stonework dates from the reign of Henry II (1154–89), who built the Round Tower on the chalk mound raised by William the Conqueror.

The lord of the castle ruled his lands like a miniature kingdom. The acquisitive magnate Hugh le Despenser, whose greed flourished in the reign of Edward II in the 14th century, had more than 50 manors (estates), with 28,000 sheep, 2,000 cattle and pigs, and 200 horses. A lord's immediate subjects were those living and working in and around his castle: soldiers, officials, builders and farmers, maids and brewers, huntsmen and falconers, pastrycooks and laundresses, smiths and stable-boys. His prestige was surpassed only by the king himself, by the greatest earls and dukes, and by the Church which, besides

◀ Henry I, king of England, a statue at Lichfield Cathedral, Staffordshire. Henry, the third son of William the Conqueror, used his castles to safeguard his throne.

FEUDAL SOCIETY

In the Middle Ages a king granted land to lords, who in turn rented out parcels of land to vassals (tenants) in return for work, or in the case of knights, military service. There were about 3,000 knights in Norman England, each owing allegiance to a lord or baron, of whom there were roughly 300. In the pyramid of secular society, the king was at the top (and God's chosen ruler); beneath him were the rulers of Church (bishops) and state (barons); below them knights and freemen; and at the very bottom the peasantry or villeins, who were effectively bound to the land they were born on.

▲ Berkeley Castle has been a family home, as well as a fortress, for over 800 years.

temporal wealth, also claimed power over his soul. The number of his subjects ranged from a few dozen to hundreds, for a castle's residents often exceeded those of some local villages. Most medieval settlements, even towns, were tiny. English poll tax returns for 1377 show Bath with only 1,902 citizens; Bristol 2,445; Newcastle 2,647; York 7,248; and London, by far the biggest city in England, had a population of 23,314.

The castle was an integral part of the medieval socio-economic system loosely known as feudalism. The lands of the 'lord of the manor' produced food and raw materials; as well as fields and livestock, they contained vineyards, forests, quarries, mines, mills and fish ponds. The castle owner held lands often widely scattered, each of which must be visited from time to time, so he was often away from home; he might also be called to attend the king at court or ride off to a foreign war. Kings were even more itinerant. While few villagers strayed far from their village, medieval monarchs were almost constantly on the move, processing in state with a large retinue from castle to castle. Each royal visit created excitement, anxiety, frantic activity and expense on food, drink, accommodation and entertainment, wherever the king chose to call on his royal progress.

◀▼ Sowing seeds and carting the harvest: illustrations from the 14th-century Luttrell Psalter show seasonal farm tasks which went on in the fields surrounding every nobleman's castle.

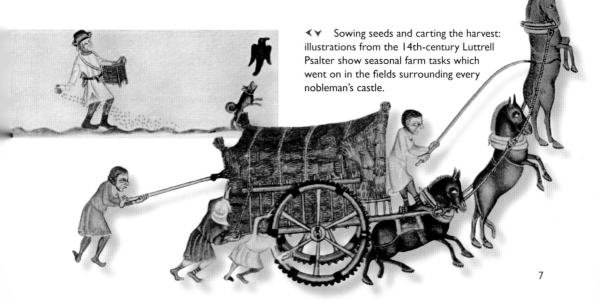

CASTLE BUILDING

The first Norman 'motte and bailey' castles sat upon artificial mounds, called mottes. On top of the mound the stockade enclosed a wooden tower and at the foot of the mound was an enclosure, the bailey, inside which were a kitchen, chapel, hall, barns, stables, stores, workshops and barracks. The bailey was ringed by an outer bank and ditch. Where they could use the foundations of Roman fortifications, the Normans built in stone – as they did at the Tower of London, Colchester and Pevensey.

As stone castles replaced the wooden castles, construction took longer and cost more. The donjon, or keep, became the focus of castle design, and gave more ample living accommodation. This main tower had several storeys: sometimes it was built on top of the motte; in other castles it was placed to bolster a weak spot, such as the gateway. Orford Castle in Suffolk had a polygonal keep, but square or rectangular keeps were more usual, with towers at the corners to provide extra strength, and clear lines of sight and firing angles for defenders.

Castle building was a specialized art; leading practitioners were in Europe-wide demand.

Edward I's castles in Wales were monumental. The king's master-builder was a Savoyard, Master James of St George, and his plan for Beaumaris Castle (1295) was the ultimate in concentric design, a series of ringed walls, each inner wall higher than the outer to give defenders the advantage over an attacking force. The walls of Conwy Castle (built in under five years from 1283) were almost a mile long; those of Caernarfon (begun in 1283) were banded in imitation of the walls of Constantinople. Caernarfon's walls are up to 5 metres (15 feet) thick, whereas elsewhere in Britain about 2 metres (6 feet) is more typical. Some medieval forts in India, by comparison, have walls 16 metres (50 feet) thick.

Castle-building employed hundreds of workers: quarrymen, labourers, masons, carpenters, smiths, carters, specialists in the arcane skills of iron-forging and chain-making, and experts in the darker arts of castle warfare, such as booby traps. Each castle's design was adapted to its site, but essential to all was a reliable water supply, usually in the form of wells. No garrison could survive a siege without water. The outer walls were

protected by earth banks, ditches and water-filled moats. The main approach was often angled to impede a mass charge by enemy soldiers and additionally fortified by an outer gatehouse or barbican. To enter the castle, attackers generally had to fight their way across a drawbridge and through at least one portcullis, an iron grille that could be lowered to seal the entrance.

Even if they overcame these obstacles, attacking soldiers would be exposed to defenders' fire in 'killing grounds' within the bailey, and bombarded through roof-openings or 'murder holes' as they penetrated internal passages. Within towers, a spiral staircase favoured the defenders; the spiral was constructed so that a defender above could swing a sword or club freely, while an attacker coming up the stairs was impeded. The most obvious wall defences were the battlements; in the 'toothed' stonework the gaps or crenels allowed archers to shoot out before taking cover behind the alternating raised portions, or merlons.

◄ Harlech Castle took seven years to build (1283–89) on a concentric plan, with inner walls much higher than outer walls. Like other English castles in Wales, it could be supplied from the sea (then much closer to the walls). A 60-metre (200-foot) fortified stairway led from the castle to the waterside.

▲ Murder holes at Bodiam: castle defenders could rain rocks and other missiles from above on an encroaching enemy. The holes might also be used by defenders to douse fires started by attackers.

▲ The Barbican at Lewes Castle in East Sussex. The purpose of a barbican was to defend the main approach and gate to a castle.

PELE TOWERS

On the borders between England and Scotland, where raiding and feuding were endemic, farmers and landowners sought safety inside pele towers. A 'pele' was a palisade, or enclosure, orginally. These fortified tower-homes had accommodation on the upper floors, beyond reach (their owners hoped) of assailants. Pele towers were built as late as the 17th century – there were nearly 100 in Cumberland alone. A walled courtyard or barmkin alongside the tower sheltered farm animals.

◄ Newark Tower near Selkirk, one of many pele (or peel) towers in the Borders region.

CASTLE HOME

▲ A 15th-century dance, with musicians playing on the balcony of the great hall to entertain the lord and his ladies.

▲ The great hall at Winchester Castle, Hampshire; the 14th-century Round Table, repainted in the reign of Henry VIII, has nothing to do with the legends of King Arthur that so influenced the art and imagination of the Middle Ages.

Even when the realm was rocked by dynastic squabble and civil war most people in the Middle Ages lived in relative peace, hearing little of the outside world; news travelled slowly and even civil wars could pass by a village without the inhabitants being much concerned by the quarrels of great lords. At home and at peace, the lord and his family enjoyed a standard of living far more comfortable than that of his workers, though his home life was spartan by modern standards and certainly less hygiene-conscious.

Instead of sharing off-duty hours with his retainers like his Norman ancestor, a Plantagenet nobleman of the 12th or 13th centuries could retire to his solar, a private room or suite of rooms. There he, his wife, children and other relatives such as widowed mothers or unmarried sisters were attended throughout the day by servants, while officials came and went about castle business – among them the chamberlain, who was in charge of the treasury, a chest full of money and jewels.

The great hall was the centre of castle activity. Here the lord was the gracious host when receiving visitors, the attentive counsellor when hearing complaints from farmers, and the stern judge when handing out punishments to law-breakers. In the hall people sat, slept, played with their dogs (ladies had small lap-dogs, men usually kept several hounds, including

▲ A 15th-century carved wooden stool, now in the V&A Museum, London. Benches and stools were the most common form of castle seating, and oak was most often used in furniture-making.

greyhounds), ate and drank, told stories, and were entertained by jesters, acrobats and minstrels. The only room matching it for importance was the chapel; prayer was part of daily life and even a battle-scarred baron usually deferred to an abbot or a bishop.

In the domestic rooms walls were plastered and whitewashed with 'plaster of Paris' from France or English gypsum. A rich man showed off his wealth by hanging his walls with painted cloths and woven tapestries; these could be taken down when he moved to another residence. Castle rooms were seldom sunny, for windows on lower walls were little more than narrow slits; upper-floor windows were larger, but still protected by iron bars and wooden shutters. Shutters or blinds of oiled cloth also kept out draughts and rain. Glass windows were costly and some castle-owners had removable glass panes, carried from home to home.

The castle kitchen was usually in a separate building; there were toilets but no bathroom; storage space consisted mainly of wooden wardrobes, cupboards and chests, along with stone niches or aumbries used as small cupboards; furniture included wooden tables, chairs, stools and beds. Three-legged stools were particularly useful on uneven floors.

Water from the well, and from rainwater cisterns, was piped around the castle in tiled culverts and lead pipes. Drinking water, unless from a spring or clean well, was often fouled, so when they had the option many people drank brewed ale or wine, and children were given watered-down 'small ale'. The hall floor, covered with rushes or straw, was seldom cleaned thoroughly, and not even scatterings of lavender and camomile could disguise the stench of dog, food scraps, spittle and sundry garbage. Writing in the early 1500s, the Dutch philosopher Erasmus complained that many English floors appeared to have been uncleaned for a generation.

Toilets, or garderobes, were small alcoves, with wooden seats and a drain chute to deposit waste into the moat, a convenient stream or a cesspit. Cesspits were cleaned out by a worker known as a 'gong-fermer', who carted the sewage off to manure the vegetable plot. Latrines often projected from the walls; Beaumaris Castle on Anglesey had more than 30. The lord's family used the 'privy' in their apartments, with the luxury of a basin or laver (washstand).

BATHING

A lordly chamber might have a bath, usually a wooden barrel cut in half. A knight's squire was expected to prepare his master's bath, with several sponges (to sit on as well as scrub with), and a sheet over the tub (to keep the water warm, rather than for modesty), and to 'always be careful that the door is shut'. Personal hygiene was erratic and bathing not a daily habit. King Edward IV, a handsome man by all accounts, was shaved by his barber once a week, when the royal head and feet were washed 'if he so desired'.

➤ A garderobe at Skipton Castle in North Yorkshire. Castle toilets could be private and unobtrusive, but many were communal latrines; external sewage disposal was less discreet, often emptying into ditches or cesspits.

THE DAILY ROUND

Each season brought tasks on the farm, and the medieval farmer had little time to sit and admire the beauties of nature. The lord of the manor lived a more leisured life. Servants helped him dress in the morning, warming his linen before the fire if the weather was cold. Servants brought him his breakfast, perhaps oatmeal porridge or bread and cold meat with a cup of wine or ale. His chaplain prayed for him in chapel, but the lord was expected to attend Mass (in Latin), often every day.

The working day involved meeting officials, such as the steward, to discuss the business of the estate: a peasant wants to marry off his daughter and the lord must approve the choice of husband; someone's pigs show signs of disease – a cause for concern; a notorious local outlaw has reappeared in the forest and must be hunted down; a farmer has died and by law the lord may demand a cow as death duty; a dispute over water-usage between the miller and the local monastery requires lordly arbitration. Having attended to such matters a nobleman could give himself over to relaxing activities, such as a game of quoits with his children or a discussion with a visiting mercer about what colour robe to buy. If the weather was fine he might ride out with his wife and falconer, taking their favourite birds for an afternoon's sport, or visit the deer park to see how the semi-wild fallow deer (imported by the Normans) were faring. The 14th-century poet William Langland asserted that it was perfectly proper for 'lewd [poor] men to labour and lords to hunt'. Such was the order of the world.

The castle was also a law court and penalties for wrongdoers could sometimes be more severe than spending a day locked in the pillory. In the 1330s a man could be hanged just for stealing a bale of cloth, as happened to John White, a London skinner, or for making off with a 'green hood', like Stephen Salle of Canterbury. Poaching the king's deer, even shooting the lord's pigeons, were offences punishable by death. In rare cases innocence or guilt might be decided by ordeal – such as pressing a heated iron to the flesh to see if it burned. In trial by combat the two

▲ The Luttrell family at dinner; from the 14th-century Luttrell Psalter, now in the British Library. The Lincolnshire knight Sir Geoffrey Luttrell sits with his family and two Dominican friars.

▲ A page from an early 1400s French illuminated manuscript, the *Tres Riches Heures du Duc de Berry*, shows a ploughman and fields in an idealized, well-ordered landscape.

▲ Medieval roads were usually impassable in winter, so spring was the time for military campaigns and journeys, like those of Geoffrey Chaucer's literary pilgrims, pictured here riding to the shrine of St Thomas Becket at Canterbury.

▲ The open hearth in the kitchen of the Great Tower of Dover Castle, Kent. Large iron cooking pots were used for stews and broths which could be kept simmering for days over the fire.

disputing parties fought it out with swords in the expectation that divine justice would decide the winner.

From time to time a great English lord would travel to London, perhaps to attend the king's court or to borrow money from a city merchant. He would ride over rough roads with an escort; women might also ride on horseback or jolt along in unsprung wagons. A God-fearing family might well return home from what Scottish poet William Dunbar called this 'flower of cities' with shocking tales of painted harlots, cutpurses (pickpockets) and 'fripperers' who sold cast-off clothes (frippery), and – in the 14th century – wide-eyed reports of fops parading in codpieces, with sleeves that trailed on the ground and shoes so absurdly curly-toed that they were fastened by gold chains to the wearer's knees!

NAKED AND UNASHAMED

Medieval people were not prudish, though the Church preached against wantonness and promiscuity. Men and women often slept naked, and weary servants stripped off wherever they found a place to sleep, provided it was warm. Henry VIII, in the early 1500s, found it necessary to issue orders that palace cooks and scullions (kitchen boys) were not to sleep naked beside the fire in the kitchen.

CASTLE WORKERS

The working day began at sunrise; a medieval rhyme runs 'Up at five, dine at nine, sup at five, and bed by nine'. Ploughmen drove teams of oxen, and sang to keep the beasts in good heart and so ensure a straight furrow. A stout, good-natured ox was a valued animal. So too was the 'good barking dog' of the shepherd; sheep were a vital resource in the medieval economy, especially in England with its flourishing wool trade with mainland Europe. Shepherds often slept out with their flock in all weathers. Children too were kept busy; their jobs included collecting firewood, herding swine as they foraged in woodland, and scaring hungry birds off freshly seeded fields.

⋏   A woman spinning, holding the spindle in her right hand and the distaff in the other. Spinning and weaving were essential household skills within the castle community.

Women and children shared such tasks as making butter and cheese, feeding poultry and tending vegetables. Women made cloth, and clothing, and almost every woman could spin wool, using distaff and spindle. The distaff was held under one arm, often with its end tucked into the woman's belt, while she plucked strands of wool from the hank at its top; the strands were fed to the dangling weighted spindle, which was spun with her other hand to twist the wool into yarn. Weaving, embroidery and basket-making were other tasks routinely carried out by women.

The steward, or seneschal, was the estate manager, usually in daily contact with his lordly master. Food and drink were the responsibility of the butler (wines), cook and pantler (bread). Security was left to the constable whenever the lord was away, and the marshal had charge of horses. A very rich lord might dress his servants in livery, a uniform dress or badge which denoted the bond between master and servant. Like a heraldic 'coat of arms' it was a status symbol, identifying the master as a person of note. In the 14th and 15th centuries the practice led to

⋏   The castle family, its retainers and soldiers were fed by the daily toil of field-workers, like this 15th-century gardener busy with his leeks.

In many ways a castle was self-sufficient. Workers made much of what was needed, such as nets and traps for hunting, as shown in this 15th-century manuscript illustration.

frequent legal wrangles about who was entitled to grant a livery, and who was not.

Craftworkers formed guilds to protect the mysteries of their crafts. Certain skills were always in demand around a castle, which needed stonemasons, sawyers, carpenters, fletchers (arrow-makers) and blacksmiths. Also kept busy were roofers – thatchers, tilers and plumbers (lead-workers) who fixed lead pipes and laid lead sheets for rain-proof roofing. A castle used a lot of ironwork too, including bars and clamps used in construction, and locks for doors and chests, but much of the smith's time at his forge was spent making and repairing tools such as axes, ploughshares, spades and chisels, and preparing swords and other weapons for the battlefield. In overall charge of the building work on castle or church was a master mason, assisted by other 'masters' such as painters, engineers and 'diggers', each of whom directed his own workforce. The master mason was the equivalent of an architect; one of the best known was Henry Yevele (c.1320–1400), whose work included the Bloody Tower in London.

THE BLACKSMITH

Despite their skills in forging and crafting iron into anything from a ploughshare to a battleaxe, the muscular blacksmith was often the butt of jokes, presumably because wags thought strength of arm could not be matched by speed of thought. A 1350 verse makes fun of smiths as 'pug-faced bumpkins', pumping away at the bellows 'till their brains are all bursting' and driving people to distraction with the 'din of their dints' [hammering].

Kitchenware, medieval style, in pottery and metal. Pottery, often made locally, varied from the cheap and plain to glazed decorated jugs and beakers. A good iron knife was a prized possession.

FAMILY LIFE

While the Church held that woman was the 'weaker vessel', and it was without doubt a man's world, a few women in medieval society lived fairly independently, ran businesses and could exert considerable influence – especially if they were queens. Eleanor of Aquitaine, a powerful woman in her own right through her land-holdings, married first the king of France (Louis VII), then the king of England (Henry II). At a more modest social level, the wife of a castle lord took charge of affairs while he was away, in France perhaps or even on crusade to the Holy Land (which might mean an absence of years, if he ever returned at all). An unmarried woman could own property, but on marriage her property passed to her husband. Many marriages were arranged to bring together lands and cement dynastic alliances, and girls were sometimes betrothed as children – often to spouses they had not yet met.

Fertile women were blessed, or burdened, with large families – ten or more children was not uncommon, though infant mortality was high. For lordly children there was plenty of

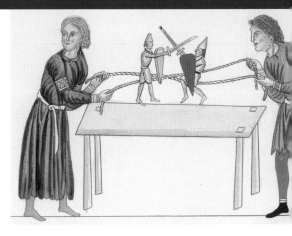

▲ Just as today, war games were popular in medieval times.

amusement playing up and down castle stairs or riding out into field and forest. Schooling was provided by monks; most noble-born boys and some girls were taught to read, at least haltingly, by monks or nuns, and girls learned from their mothers the arts of domesticity. Few poor children were given much schooling, though a bright poor boy might be noticed and be taught by monks, in preparation for a monastic life.

When not busy with maternal duties, even rich women passed the time in household tasks such as spinning and embroidery. Servants helped the lord and lady to get dressed, and the castle laundresses were kept busy washing clothes on fine days. A lady's day dress, or kirtle, was laced at the front, with a belt from which to hang her rosary beads, keys and a purse. Beneath was a shift, like a long shirt. Her woollen stockings were held up by garters, and her leather shoes were protected by wooden pattens (wooden under-shoes) if she went out on a wet day.

Poor people wore much the same all year round, usually a coarse woollen tunic and long stockings for men, and a long dress for women. Boots and shoes were optional. Children wore hand-me-downs and were dressed as smaller versions of their parents. For winter warmth,

▲ English leather shoes. The long pointed-toe style was fashionable in the late 14th century. Castle footwear was usually more functional.

the wealthy put on colourful cloaks and thick furs of squirrel, sable, fox or wolf. The poor wrapped and hooded themselves against wind and rain in old sacks and tattered sheepskins.

Women's hair, usually plaited and pinned, was, from the late 12th century, often concealed beneath a wimple – a band of cloth around the head and chin held in place by a stiff linen crown. Fashions became more extravagant by the 15th century, when men's doublets (short coats with padded fronts) and tight-fitting hose caused outraged clerics to lament that such peacocks looked 'more like to tormentors or devils in their clothing than to men'.

∧ Gentlewomen washing their hair and attending to their complexions, from a 15th-century French manuscript in Glasgow University Library.

GRACIOUS LIVING

If the comforts of the castle's domestic quarters seemed exotic to the cottager, the scale of the great hall was intimidating, with its high roof, carved stone hearth, tapestried walls – and gazing down upon all, the lord and master on his dais. The most splendid castles matched the royal palaces. Castles today strike us as cold and draughty, and many probably were, even in their prime. It takes a leap of imagination, or a computer visual, to paint bare walls, replace ceilings and floors where there are now gaping joist-holes in stonework, and position curtains and screens to partition what now seem empty, even gloomy spaces. Cavernous vaults and dark passages rang with the sound of voices and scurrying feet, glowed with light from oil lamps and torches, and smelled of food, wine, perfumes, spices, wood smoke – pleasant aromas

to mask the doubtless less attractive odours from the drains.

The lord's bedroom was a world away from a poor family's wattle and daub thatched hut, where everyone slept more or less in a huddle, and a bed was a luxury – many sleeping on the floor on straw, rushes or sheepskins. Castle living aimed for more elegance; the English scholar Alexander of Neckam (1157–1217) wrote that a nobleman's bedchamber should have curtains or canopies 'for the avoiding of flies and spiders'. The bed curtains also helped to keep out draughts and provide some privacy for its occupants. Privacy was a rare privilege in the Middle Ages, enjoyed by very few. A nobleman's bed had a feather mattress, with a bolster and pillow, sheets of muslin, cotton or linen, and covers of woollen cloth lined with

◄ A well-to-do couple in their bedroom, about 1475, when the austerely furnished castles of the Middle Ages were evolving into more comfortable great homes.

fur – comfortable enough if you could forget the bugs and lice which abounded in the beds of rich and poor alike.

Castle heating came from portable braziers and log fires, though coal was also burned; in older buildings the smoke drifted up to blacken the roof beams before escaping. Fireplaces were set against an outer wall, with a hole or flue to carry away the smoke and a stone-built hood over the fireplace. The hood looked like a woman's cloak or mantle – hence 'mantelpiece'. Chimneys were rare before the 15th century, when brick chimney stacks came into general use on fortified manor houses, the preferred homes of a new generation of wealthy landowners and merchants.

The castle garden was a place for relaxation and enjoyment. Many gardens copied the good practice of monastic gardens, where monks grew medicinal herbs as well as fruit trees, vines and vegetables. In a castle garden people could

to take the air, gossip and exchange 'sweet nothings', for the medieval ideal of courtly love, conveyed through poetry and ballad, inspired the notion of the garden as a 'pleasaunce' (pleasure-ground) where love ruled. Gardens, such as Queen Eleanor's Garden at Winchester Castle (Hampshire), were laid out in formal designs, with hedges, paths, arbors, fountains and ponds, and flower beds in which lilies, marigolds, roses and gillyflowers bloomed.

WARRENS AND PIGEON-HOUSES

Rabbits, known as coneys, were kept in warrens or 'coneygarths'. The Normans brought the rabbit to Britain, as a table delicacy and for its fur; regarded as delicate warm-climate creatures, rabbits were kept in enclosed warrens and caught by the warrener using nets and ferrets. Escapees from warrens established Britain's wild rabbit population. The Normans also introduced pigeon-houses, or dovecotes, often housing hundreds of nests. The pigeon-keeper, or culverer, climbed up a ladder to harvest the young birds for the table.

➤ This ancient dovecot at Dunster in Somerset has been altered and repaired over the centuries. A dovecot is thought to have stood here since the 14th century, when it belonged to the local Benedictine priory. Doves made a welcome addition to the medieval dinner table.

▲ Queen Eleanor's Garden at Winchester Castle. As well as a place to sit and walk, castle gardens could provide herbs and spices for medicines and the kitchen.

FESTIVE FOOD

L avish entertainments were laid on if the king came visiting, and in proportion for callers of lower rank. Feasts also marked special religious holy days or a happy family event, such as the birth of a son and heir, but the medieval Christmas was a more solemn, wholly religious occasion – though people still enjoyed the old midwinter festivities of play-acting, singing and dancing. On special occasions the castle's outer enclosure was covered with tents and temporary wooden buildings for use as lodgings, extra kitchens or storage.

Dinner was usually eaten early, about 10 a.m., with supper between 5 and 6 p.m. In the hall, the lord and his lady sat at the high table looking down on everyone else and sharing this eminence with a select few: churchmen, noblemen, family members. The table had a linen tablecloth. Other guests sat 'below the high table' on benches set along wooden trestle tables. The 'sideboard' was simply another table, used for plates and dishes.

Since the kitchen was some distance away from the hall, it is likely that hot food was often tepid by the time it reached the table. The buttery provided wines and ale; the pantry bread; the poultry game and domestic fowl; the cartilage fruit and vegetables; the napery table linen; the saucery spices and sauces; and the scullery eating and cooking utensils. The larderer and cellarer were responsible, to the steward, for feeding as many as 100 or more guests – which might mean roasting two or three oxen and the preparation of an assortment of meats, pies, puddings and fruits.

Scullions or kitchen servants were kept hard at work by the cook, who also chivvied the sweating spit-boy turning the roasting spit on which sizzled the beef, pork, venison, geese and capons. Salt meat, preserved in barrels, had to be slowly boiled in a large cauldron suspended from a brandreth, or tripod, over the fire.

Servants scurried to and fro, bearing dishes of food and jugs of wine. The lord was always

FIT FOR A FEAST

Cooks prepared elaborate dishes for a feast, such as partridge stewed in beef broth with spices, served on bread with a dressing of ginger and hard-boiled eggs, or 'wafer of pike' (the belly of the fish, cooked, mixed with cheese, then served on biscuit wafers made from flour and egg white). Pride of place might go to a swan or peacock roasted and then sewn back into its skin, complete with feathers.

◄ Castle interiors were often handsomely decorated, and came alive on festive occasions. This illustration from a British Library manuscript shows a state banquet, as the king of Portugal and John of Gaunt, son of Edward III of England, dine diplomatically to celebrate a marriage.

► Fine glass was reserved for the castle lord's table. A goblet like this one, now held in the Museum of London, might have been bought from a London merchant during a nobleman's visit to the city.

served first and, if wary of murderous enemies, had his portion tasted by a servant in case of poison. Diners brought their own knives, and ate with their fingers and spoons. Two or more people shared the same plate, and thick trenchers of bread made tasty serving dishes, the bread absorbing the juices. Guests helped themselves to small loaves called manchets to sop up the gravy. Forks were not common before the 16th century, though Piers Gaveston, favourite of King Edward II, reportedly owned silver forks 'for eating pears'. Tableware included wooden bowls, pewter dishes, beakers made of leather or horn and, rarely, costly glass. The chief table ornament was the salt cellar, often in silver, which was set in front of the principal guest. The nef, a model ship filled with spices, was another highlight of the rich man's table. The wassail bowl for drinking toasts was called the mazer; made of maple wood, the bowl was lidded and richly decorated.

▲ Most work in a castle kitchen was carried out by men. This artist's reconstruction shows a busy scene as cooks prepare meat in the kitchen at Old Wardour Castle in Wiltshire. The castle was built in the late 14th century for the 5th Lord Lovel.

◄ Ceramics from the 14th century. Huge amounts of domestic pottery were made, used, broken and thrown away. These examples are in the Museum of London.

TABLE MANNERS

Dogs might gnaw on bones tossed to them from the table, but medieval manners were not unrefined. It was not done to scratch, nor talk with your mouth full, nor blow your nose with your fingers – best use the corner of your robe. Grace was said before and after meals, and servants carried in water and napkins for guests to wash their hands. In his *Book of Nurture*, John Russell advised young squires to place the salt at their lord's right hand, with on his left side 'knife and spoon folded in a napkin'. He also warned them never to lick the dust from a bowl to make it look clean!

The castle garrison was usually small, perhaps 20 to 30 men, usually enough to defend a well-built castle until help arrived. The soldiers' main tasks were to guard the walls, watch over prisoners, and patrol the countryside to maintain the king's peace and see that the poor paid their taxes.

The elite fighters of medieval warfare were knights and other men-at-arms (professional soldiers) who rode in full armour on horses. Knights fought with swords, axes, lances and formidable-looking clubs or maces, and their role on the battlefield was as heavy cavalry, smashing gaps in enemy ranks by the sheer weight of the

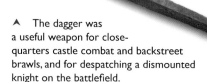

⋏ The dagger was a useful weapon for close-quarters castle combat and backstreet brawls, and for despatching a dismounted knight on the battlefield.

charge (more of a trot than a gallop). The main weapons to counter horsemen was the bow, but infantry soldiers carried polearms such as spears, halberds and poleaxes which could unseat a rider – giving the foot-soldier time to rush in and finish him off with a dagger. Archers were essential to a castle's defence, since a longbow had a range of 400 metres (400 yards) and a good archer could shoot more than ten arrows a minute. The crossbow was slower-firing but effective when shot from the castle walls, being accurate and penetrating, and 'great crossbows' with a span of 2 metres (6 feet) were also used as wall-mounted light artillery.

Knights were attended by youthful squires, whose main duty was to serve their lord and master and look after horses and weapons. A squire was also expected to have social skills; the poet Geoffrey Chaucer wrote that a squire should be able to make songs and poems, joust and dance, draw and write. Boys as young as 7

THE ARCHER

The longbow was usually made from yew wood. It was as long as a man was tall, and the typical pull was 90kg (200lb). An archer usually carried 24 arrows of 'clothyard' length (0.9m/3 ft), and would change arrowheads depending on whether he was shooting deer or men – a thin bodkin point could pierce armour. The armoury needed to maintain a large supply of arrows since archers defending a castle could not easily retrieve shot arrows – though they could reuse those shot into the castle by the enemy.

⋏ Archers fought in almost every medieval battle. This selection of arrowheads, in the Museum of London, shows different shapes for different purposes including hunting and piercing armour.

⋎ Archers practising with longbows – an essential part of military training. One at least has hit the mark. This picture comes from the 14th-century Luttrell Psalter in the British Library.

▲ The giant crossbow, similar to the Roman ballista, fired a heavy bolt easily capable of felling a man in armour. Crossbows, giant or conventional, required less strength and skill to use than a longbow, and were useful defensive weapons in a castle.

➤ The knight's principal weapon was his sword. This is the tomb of William Marshal, 2nd Earl of Pembroke (died 1231), with sword and shield, in the Temple Church, London. His father, William Marshal, the 1st Earl, was a famous knight who won the favour of King Henry II, and held numerous castles including Pembroke, Chepstow and Kilkenny.

left home to serve as pages. At about 14 they became squires, and at 21 or older a squire might be dubbed knight. He would have trained to joust and fight in armour, and absorbed at least the basic ideals of chivalry.

Armour developed from the chain mail of the Normans to the 14th-century bodysuit of steel plates. This weighed around 25kg (55lb) – sabbatons for the feet, greaves for the leg below the knee, cuisses on the thighs, breech (short mail skirt), breastplate, pauldrons on the shoulders, vambraces and rerebraces on the arms, gauntlets for the hands and a bascinet (helmet). Thus equipped, knights rode into battle on chargers or destriers. The destrier was a muscular mount, strong enough to carry a knight, his armour and the horse's own armour (chanfron on the head, mail skirts to protect the legs and flanks) which added an additional 30kg (65lb). Over this protection, a warhorse wore an embroidered cloth, or caparison, bearing the heraldic devices of its owner. Castle stables also housed light riding horses, or palfreys, while heavy carthorses and packhorses were kept for transport and farm work.

In time of war, a garrison grew into a small army, as the lord called on his vassals to fulfil their feudal duty. In the 14th century every man aged 15 to 40 who had land and goods worth £15 was required to turn out with armour, weapons and a horse. The poor were instructed to bring whatever weapons they could, such as billhooks, pitchforks, staves and 'bowes and arrows out of the forest'.

CASTLES AT WAR

Many castles enjoyed a comparatively peaceful existence, while others were the scenes of frequent battles, usually small-scale. Foreign wars, such as Henry V's campaigns in France, affected few ordinary folk at home, except that taxation went up to pay for them. Local wars such as the Wars of the Roses, or those between Scots and English, could affect local populations far more, but often skirted around castles. Most medieval battles were bloody hand-to-hand fights in the open between

> Steps lead up to this slit – just wide enough for an archer's arrow – in the walls at Kenilworth Castle, Warwickshire. In 1266 this castle was the setting for one of the most celebrated sieges in English history.

COATS OF ARMS

Fighting in a castle or on the battlefield, a knight in armour needed to tell friend from foe. Badges and family colours worn on shields and cloth surcoats evolved into 'coats of arms', with patterns and devices denoting the wearer, and gave rise to the rules of heraldry.

⋏ John of Gaunt displays his decorative surcoat – literally a 'coat of arms' – to tell the world who he is.

armies whose leaders were intent on deciding the issue in a day. Locals kept away until it was time to loot the corpses.

A castle's defenders could usually fight off a direct attack, provided their fortifications had been properly maintained. From machicolations, fighting platforms built out from the castle walls, they could drop rocks, boiling liquids and other missiles, while archers shot arrows through narrow windows (arrow-loops). Raiding parties rushed forth from small gates called sally-ports to surprise the enemy. The main threats to the castle walls came from stone-throwing 'engines', battering rams and movable siege towers. Scaling ladders were easier to push away with long poles.

If a determined enemy force settled down to besiege a castle, a struggle lasting weeks or months might ensue. At Rochester Castle in 1215, Kentish rebels defied King John for two months; the defenders held out until, reduced to eating their horses, they were forced to surrender.

In 1266, during the 'Barons' War', Henry III attacked Kenilworth Castle where the supporters of the rebel baron Simon de Montfort (killed at Evesham the year before) were holed up. Kenilworth defied even heavy catapults hauled up from London and thwarted attempts by Henry's soldiers to cross its mere by barge. In the end the king summoned the Archbishop of Canterbury to stand outside the castle walls and pronounce excommunication on the defenders.

◀ An English Heritage reconstruction of the siege of Dover Castle, 1216. The assault lasted, with a short truce, into 1217, and involved siege engines (possibly the first use of a trebuchet in England), a wooden siege tower and undermining operations.

SIEGE ENGINES

Medieval siege engines were used as artillery. The mangonel worked by torsion: it was 'wound up' by twisting ropes which drew back the throwing arm; when the tension was released the arm flew forward, flinging a stone. The trebuchet was a counterweight engine, with a weighted beam on a pivot. When released, the loaded end flew up into the air projecting its missile (usually a stone but sometimes a human corpse or dead animal) over the walls of a castle. Smaller arrow-firing artillery, known as espringals or scorpions, were based on designs used since Roman times.

They were unrepentant. After six months it was starvation and sickness, not the fear of perdition, that forced them to yield.

In Wales, Harlech Castle endured a winter siege by Madoc ap Llywelyn in 1294, surviving on supplies brought in by sea. In 1404 the English-held fortress fell to Owain Glyndwr after starvation and sickness reduced the garrison to 21 men, but it was recaptured after an eight-month siege by Prince Henry (the future Henry V). Harlech endured further years of siege during the Wars of the

Roses; in 1468, it was the last Lancastrian stronghold to surrender, an epic that by tradition inspired the song 'Men of Harlech'. Sieges could sometimes be as deadly to the attacker as to the defender. Scotland's James II was killed in 1460 when a cannon blew up during his siege of Roxburgh Castle, in the Borders region.

▼ Edinburgh Castle has seen many battles in its long history. In 1314, the Earl of Moray (nephew of Robert the Bruce) captured the castle with just 30 soldiers. The Scots climbed the rocky mount and castle walls under cover of darkness, and surprised the English garrison.

DEATH AND DISEASE

Most castle dwellers were well-muscled through hard work, military training and outdoor activity – only sedentary priests needed keep-fit advice such as 'strutting or swinging vigorously' from a knotted rope fastened to a roof beam.

However, life in the Middle Ages could be nasty, brutish and short. People lived with the knowledge of mortality, of which they were constantly reminded by the Church and by the yearly toll of injury, sickness, old age and disease.

Medicine was a mixture of folklore, herbals, a bit of practical surgery, and magic. One 14th-century treatment for quinsy, a throat infection, suggested the following: kill, skin and gut a fat cat, then stuff it 'as you stuff a goose' with a mixture of hedgehog and bear grease, sage, honeysuckle gum and the herb fenugreek; roast the cat, collect the dripping and rub it on the patient. Recommended palliatives for toothache, ascribed to 'worms' in the teeth, were myrrh and opium. A more dramatic cure was to use a candle made from mutton fat and sea holly: the patient had to hold the lighted candle as close as possible to the affected tooth, with a basin of water beneath it; the 'tooth-worms' would drop into the water, to escape the heat of the candle!

In the modern mind castles are often associated with torture chambers and dungeons but in fact few were consistently used as prisons. A common thief awaiting trial before the baronial court might be locked in the castle cellar, but imprisonment was not a routine punishment, unlike execution which was far more common.

▲ Richard II of England lost his throne to a usurper, Henry Bolingbroke (Henry IV), and died in Pontefract Castle in West Yorkshire.

Notable prisoners, usually those unfortunate or foolish enough to have picked the losing side in a royal or baronial squabble, might be kept locked up for years, sometimes in relative comfort but often in darkness, damp and squalor. The worst fate was to be cast into the oubliette – a dark pit in which the miserable captive was simply forgotten, but kept alive with scraps tossed in by a gaoler. Few medieval gaolers would have shrunk from using torture, but this too was probably less common than we might imagine – though the rack, on which the victim was stretched until he confessed or his limbs broke, is said to have been devised by a constable of the Tower of London.

Among famous royal castle prisoners were Edward II, who in 1327 died at Berkeley Castle, almost certainly murdered, and Richard II who died in 1400 at Pontefract Castle, either by foul play or starvation. The Tower of London incarcerated many, often undeserving of their fate. Among those who met their deaths there were the Princes in the Tower, Edward V and his brother, who are presumed to have been murdered in 1483. The Tower's most horrible cell was Little Ease, so small that the prisoner inside could neither stand nor lie full length.

➤ Medieval justice could be brutal. A miscreant, or an ousted rival for power, might be hanged or beheaded. Penalties for lesser offences included branding, having an ear cut off, or spending a day in the pillory, as shown here.

◀ The Tower of London has been the scene of imprisonment, torture and painful death for many famous people throughout history.

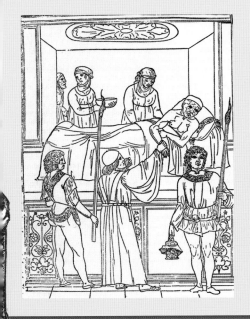

THE BLACK DEATH

The Black Death was a Europe-wide epidemic, probably of bubonic plague, that struck Britain in 1348, killing as many as one third of the population and leaving hundreds of villages desolate. The Church was left stricken, and no castle was a safe refuge from the 'great mortality'. Yet castles remained a spending priority, and from 1350 Edward III embarked on a costly rebuilding programme at Windsor Castle.

◀ A plague victim waits for death. Margaret Paston of Norfolk lost her son John to the plague in London in 1479. His death is recorded in one of the 'Paston Letters', a treasury of 15th-century correspondence. The Pastons inherited Caister Castle from their neighbour, Sir John Fastolf (died 1459), though only after fighting off other claimants.

ENTERTAINMENT

When at ease, the castle family entertained itself indoors with games of various kinds, including cards – playing cards first appeared in Europe in the 14th century. Chess had been played in England since King Cnut's reign in the 11th century, but even this pastime could become tense: a chess game between the Black Prince and the captive Philip of France almost ended in blows, until courtiers diplomatically ceded the disputed piece to their prisoner.

In great houses, minstrels sang and played to entertain guests. Musical instruments were many and varied, including viol, trumpet, harp, bagpipes, tambourine, pipe and tabor, and nakers (drums). Minstrels travelled the country,

⌄   Musicians entertain while a couple enjoy a game of chess; from a 14th-century German manuscript.

carrying news from castle to town, and made up rhymes about current events. When John Ball preached insurgency in 1381 at the time of the Peasants' Revolt, he took as his text the lines of a popular song: 'When Adam delved and Eve span/ Who was then the gentleman?'

Almost everyone danced, and not just on May Day; Edward I had a favourite dancer named Matilda Makejoy, who possibly shed her clothes during the performance. People laughed at rather bawdy jokes too, and jesters or fools were granted considerable licence to take liberties at their master's expense. Drama was staged in the open air on temporary stages and was largely confined to religious stories, such as the mystery, morality and miracle plays, though with plenty of action and special effects which kept the audience spellbound.

Hunting was the sport of kings, who set aside large areas as royal hunting forests where they chased deer and boar with spear and bow. Royal household accounts from the 1130s list various huntsmen, including hornblowers, fewterers (who kept greyhounds), the leader of the lime-hound (a leashed hound released to kill a stag at bay), and wolf-hunters. Hawking was enjoyed by both sexes; trained falcons were highly prized and housed in mews. Castle bedchambers often had a perch for a favourite falcon.

➢   A falconer and his hawk take part in a display at Alnwick Castle, Northumberland. Falconry was a popular medieval sport and a castle lord employed his own falconers.

Jousting was often portrayed in a fictional setting, as in this 15th-century picture which shows the knights Tristan and Palamedes in combat at the mythical court of King Arthur.

A stag hunt in progress. Kings set aside royal forests for hunting, and most castle lords had hounds and huntsmen at their command.

ROBUST SPORTS

The medieval taste in sport was for blood: cockfights, bull-baiting and bear-baiting were common. Football was a violent free-for-all. Popular contests included tilting with lances from boats in a fast-flowing river, stone-heaving, javelin-throwing, wrestling and archery competitions. In winter people took to the ice using 'the shin-bones of beasts' for skates and propelling themselves along frozen rivers with iron-shod poles.

The tournament became popular from the 11th century, despite disapproval from the Church and at first the monarch. Henry II of England tried to ban these mock battles but his son Richard I was an enthusiast, and licensed tournaments thereafter enjoyed royal patronage. Crowds gathered to enjoy the pitched battle, or mêlée, and the rough and tumble of jousting between mounted knights with lances. A 1292 statute ruled that swords must not be death-sharp and blunt-ended lances also reduced the risk of serious injury, but even so deaths still occurred; in 1344 William Montagu, 1st Earl of Salisbury died from jousting wounds, and his grandson later died jousting at Windsor – allegedly killed by his own father.

Accidents were not confined only to combatants; in 1347 Queen Philippa, wife to King Edward III of England, tumbled to earth with her ladies when their wooden pavilion, the equivalent of a modern stadium stand, collapsed while they were watching the jousting. The queen was praised for asking that no carpenter be punished.

CASTLE TO STATELY HOME

Foreign threats and civil war ensured the survival of the castle into the 1500s, and beyond, but cannon and the changing nature of warfare had altered military priorities. In 1464, during the Wars of the Roses, the fall of Bamburgh Castle in Northumberland signalled that castles were not impregnable against a 'battering train'; three great 'bombard' guns named London, Newcastle and Dijon assailed Bamburgh's walls, along with smaller guns.

Cannon alone, however, were not the nemesis of the castle. Society changed as economic power shifted to the towns. A king now needed merchants' money more than he needed armoured knights and bowmen. Noble families turned castles into showpieces, like Warwick Castle, home of the de Beauchamp earls from 1268. By the early 15th century a castle might even serve as a retirement home, as did Caister Castle in Norfolk, acquired by the Agincourt veteran Sir John Fastolf (who was perhaps a model for Shakespeare's Falstaff). Some of the last castles built in Britain primarily for military use were the gun-forts of Henry VIII, such as Deal Castle in Kent (1539–40) with its artillery bastions to bombard enemy ships; others of this type were Walmer (Kent), Portland (Dorset) and St Mawes (Cornwall).

Increasingly, castellated austerity gave way to comfort, fortified manor houses replacing fortresses. The 13th-century Stokesay Castle in Shropshire is one example; another is Brodie Castle in Moray, begun about 1560. Many castles retained a military use as garrisons through the English Civil War of the 1600s. Caerlaverock Castle in Dumfries and Galloway, one of the finest medieval castles in Scotland, survived dismantling by Robert the Bruce only to be again reduced by the Covenanters in the 1600s. By 1700 many castles had been 'slighted' (part-demolished) and abandoned, their stones carted away by local farmers and builders.

The 19th-century interest in the Gothic-style revived architectural interest in castles – leading to restoration of some and the creation of new castles as 'stately homes'. In the 1870s William Burges created the mock-medieval fantasy Castell Coch, north-west of Cardiff. In Scotland, Brodick Castle on the Isle of Arran, dating from the 13th century and extended in the 17th century by Oliver Cromwell, was in 1844 renovated in Victorian style.

Many smaller medieval buildings inevitably disappeared over the centuries as towns were remodelled and the countryside changed.

The most visible reminders of that vanished age are the cathedrals, churches and castles that still stand, great monuments in stone to the lives of their builders. Some are half-forgotten, ruined skeletons of masonry, home only to nesting birds. Many castles, in public and private

▲ Modern jousters clash during a re-enactment tournament in Scotland. Such displays demand skill, training and athleticism, recapturing the colour and energy of life in a medieval castle.

▼ Warwick Castle, reflected peacefully in the calm water of the River Avon. Castles such as Warwick were often at the centre of turbulent struggles for power during the Middle Ages.

▲ Hever Castle in Kent; the oldest part of the castle dates from the late 1200s. Converted to a manor house in the 1460s, Hever was the home of Anne Boleyn, second wife to Henry VIII.

▼ Caerlaverock Castle in south-west Scotland. Edward I laid siege to the castle in 1300. It was then dismantled by Sir Eustace Maxwell to deny it to the English, but much of the original masonry and gatehouse survives.

▼ Stokesay Castle in Shropshire is a splendid example of the castle's evolution into a fortified manor house. This view from the north shows the tower walls, with the hall beyond.

ownership, have taken on new roles as heritage centres, recreational and business enterprises, and museums. With re-enactments and other events, they have come alive once again to recreate the magic and mysteries of life in the Middle Ages.

PLACES TO VISIT

The British Isles is fortunate in having a rich medieval heritage, despite the many changes in social and economic conditions over time. There are castles across England, Wales, Scotland and Ireland to interest and delight the visitor. Some are in public ownership and others are privately owned, but most are open to the public for at least some days in the year. Here are contact details for a selection of just some places that are well worth a visit.

Alnwick Castle, Alnwick, Northumberland NE66 1NQ
01665 510777; www.alnwickcastle.com

Arundel Castle, Arundel, West Sussex BN18 9AB
01903 882173; www.arundelcastle.org/_pages/01_castle.htm

Cahir Castle, Castle Street, Cahir, Co. Tipperary
+353 52 7441011; www.heritageireland.ie/en/South-East/CahirCastle

Cardiff Castle, Castle Street, Cardiff, South Glamorgan CF10 3RB
029 2087 8100; www.cardiffcastle.com

Carrickfergus Castle, Carrickfergus, Co. Antim BT38 7BG
028 9335 1273; www.ni-environment.gov.uk

Colchester Castle, Castle Park, Colchester, Essex CO1 1TJ
01206 282939; www.colchestermuseums.org.uk and follow the link

Duart Castle, Isle of Mull, Argyll PA64 6AP
01680 812 309; www.duartcastle.com

Dunvegan Castle, Dunvegan, Isle of Skye IV55 8WF
01470 521206; www.dunvegancastle.com/content/default.asp

Hever Castle, Hever, Kent TN8 7NG
01732 865224; www.hevercastle.co.uk

Leeds Castle, near Maidstone, Kent ME17 1PB
01622 765400; www.leeds-castle.com

Lincoln Castle, Castle Hill, Lincoln, Lincolnshire LN1 3AA
01522 511068; www.lincolnshire.gov.uk

Manorbier Castle, Manorbier, Pembrokeshire SA70 7TD
01834 871394; www.manorbiercastle.co.uk

Pembroke Castle, Pembroke, Pembrokeshire SA71 4LA
01646 684585; www.pembroke-castle.co.uk

Tower of London, Tower Hill, London EC3N 4AB
020 7488 5663; www.hrp.org.uk/toweroflondon

Warwick Castle, Warwick, Warwickshire CV34 4QU
0871 265 2000; www.warwick-castle.co.uk

Winchester Castle and Queen Eleanor's Garden, The Great Hall, The Castle, Winchester, Hampshire SO23 8PJ
01962 846476; www3.hants.gov.uk/greathall

Windsor Castle, Windsor, Berkshire SL4 1NJ
020 7766 7304; www.royalcollection.org.uk and follow the link

Caernarfon Castle, Caernarfon, Gwynedd LL552AY
01286 677617; www.cadw.wales.gov.uk and follow the Places to Visit link

Caerphilly Castle, Caerphilly, Gwent CF83 1JD
029 2088 3143; www.cadw.wales.gov.uk and follow the Places to Visit link

ENGLISH HERITAGE

Dover Castle, Castle Hill, Dover, Kent CT16 1HU
01304 211067; www.english-heritage.org.uk/dovercastle

Kenilworth Castle, Kenilworth, Warwickshire CV8 1NE
01926 852078; www.english-heritage.org.uk/kenilworthcastle

Doune Castle, Castle Road, Doune, Stirling FK16 6EA
01786 841742; www.historic-scotland.gov.uk

Edinburgh Castle, Castlehill, Edinburgh EH1 2NG
0131 225 9846; www.edinburghcastle.gov.uk

National Trust

Bodiam Castle, Bodiam, East Sussex TN32 5UA
01580 830196; www.nationaltrust.org.uk

Dunster Castle, Dunster, Somerset TA24 6SL
01643 823004; www.nationaltrust.org.uk

Information correct at time of going to press.

BACKGROUND: Lincoln Castle, built by William the Conqueror.